Marking Time

A comedy

Michael Snelgrove

Samuel French — London
New York - Toronto - Hollywood

ISBN 0 573 01828 6

Please see page iv for further copyright information.

MARKING TIME

This play was first presented by the Backstage Theatre Company at the Little Theatre, Bracknell and Wokingham College on 21st November 1996. It was subsequently performed at South Hill Park Arts Centre, Bracknell, and, during November 1997, at The Man In The Moon Theatre, Chelsea, London, with the following cast:

Pat	Lin Blakley
Howard	Peter Pearson
Ian	Daniel Austin
Oliver	Jerry Radburn
Judith	Robbie Pettitt

Director Mike Snelgrove
Set designer Sue Lawson Dick
Set construction Ken Gillard
Lighting designer Chris Pettitt
Produced for the Backstage Theatre Company by David
 Edwards

CHARACTERS

Pat, mid-forties
Howard, early forties
Ian, late twenties-early thirties
Oliver, early fifties
Judith, mid-thirties

The action of the play takes place in a tiny room in a shire county's residential teachers' centre

Time—the present

This play is dedicated to the memory of
my Mum

ACT I

A tiny room in a shire county's residential teachers' centre

Part of a substantial old house, this was obviously once a place of some grandeur. Now, though, the place has a worn, but still pleasant, feel to it. There are doors L and R. The furniture was once good but is now rather tatty; there are leather armchairs with rips in, a sofa, a hatstand, a few more municipal plastic chairs, regulation school laminated tables, etc. On one of the tables is a telephone; on another, a folder of overhead projector transparencies. There are books in the room, too, among them a tatty sensational paperback and a large loose leaf book, The Compendium of Marking Guidelines

When the play begins, Pat is sitting at one of the tables, laboriously marking papers, her back towards the doors to the corridor outside. Pat is in her midforties and dresses with some chic — in pink — but with no attempt at overt trendiness or show — very much a Monsoon lady. If she were male she would be described as dapper. At her right elbow she has a formidable pile of exam papers, at her left elbow a much smaller pile. She has a pink sheet of paper — the marking band guidelines — in front of her. She is obviously a very slow but appreciative marker, passing little comments to herself as she corrects the work, tutting, cooing over a particularly pleasing passage. She finishes one paper with a flourish and a coo and puts it on the tiny pile of already marked papers. Her cheerfulness disappears as she registers the large pile of papers still to be marked near her other elbow. Wearily she takes the top one, makes a note on a mark sheet and begins the laborious process again

The door L from the corridor flies open and Howard enters, slamming it behind him. Howard is in his early forties, smallish, compact, wearing a perpetual worried frown, and the look of a man who hasn't slept much of late. He has a massive bundle of papers neatly stacked in his arms and a clipboard under one arm

Pat barely looks up — this kind of thing has obviously been going on for some time

Howard dumps his bundle of papers on one of the empty tables. He mutters something under his breath and exits again, slamming the door

Pat tries to get deeper into her marking

The door R flies open and Ian enters, slamming it behind him. He, too, carries a huge pile of papers which he dumps on another table. He is in his late twenties or early thirties: on the verge of an incredible scruffiness, pony-tailed, string in his shoes, Scottish. He, too, exits muttering, slamming the door behind him

No sooner has Ian gone than Howard enters from the L door, slamming it behind him. He carries another huge pile of papers, which he dumps and exits, slamming the door

Simultaneously, Ian enters from the door R, with more papers. He slams the door and repeats his procedure. As he is pulling the door to on this exit——

Howard enters from the door L with more papers; he slams the door, creating a double bang

Pat buries her face in her hands but tries to carry on marking

Howard dumps his papers

Ian dashes in with his latest load, slamming the door behind him. He has, in effect, "caught up" with Howard, and they exit through their various doors, muttering and slamming the doors simultaneously

There is a slight pause and then they both come in together with huge piles of papers, slamming the doors simultaneously

Pat (*throwing down her pen*) Aaaagh!
Howard What?
Ian What?
Pat Nothing. (*She returns to her marking*)
Howard (*to Ian*) Right?
Ian Right.

Howard produces his clipboard and a pen. During the following, Ian checks the piles of papers, touching each one as Howard calls out its name and ticks the list on his clipboard

Howard Dickens?
Ian Dickens.
Howard *Curiosity Shop*?

A huge pile

Ian *Curiosity Shop.*
Howard *Dorrit*?

A much smaller pile

Ian *Dorrit.*
Howard Smollett?
Ian Smollett.

A tiny pile

Howard Trollope?
Ian (*looking briefly at Pat*) Trollope.
Howard Bunyan?
Ian Bunyan.
Howard Keats?
Ian Ummm ...
Howard Keats, Keats ...?
Ian No Keats.
Howard No Keats?
Ian No Keats.
Howard Sorry. I meant Wordsworth.
Ian Ummm ...
Howard Don't tell me we've got no Wordsworth?
Pat I've got the Wordsworth.
Howard She's got the Wordsworth ...
Ian She's welcome.
Howard *All's Well.*

Ian nods and stands there

  All's Well ...

A moment passes while Ian catches up

Ian Oh sorry. I thought you meant we'd finished. (*He taps a huge pile*) *All's Well.*
Pat That ends well.
Howard Sorry?
Pat Nothing.
Ian What about the *Godots*?

Howard We're waiting for them.

Pat laughs

What?
Pat Nothing. Nothing.

Howard and Ian look at each other

Howard OK. We can shift the *Dorrits* and the Smolletts. Ian?
Ian Right. (*He picks up the two tiny piles*)
Howard They're going to Team A. Have you seen Boswell?
Ian No.
Howard Pat, have you seen Boswell?
Pat Boswell? We're not doing Boswell, are we? Is Boswell a set text?
Howard Terry Boswell.
Pat Oh, Terry Boswell. No.
Howard Bloody man.
Pat Here we go.
Howard Sorry?
Pat Nothing.
Howard The computer at Byfleet goes down, we have to do the cross-sectional referencing by hand and Terry Boswell picks this moment to go walkabouts with his entire team. On an awkwardness scale of ten, this is a nine. What are you standing around for, Ian? *Dorrits* and Smolletts to Boswell.
Ian Right.

Ian exits, pulling the door shut behind him with his foot

Howard I suppose I'd better deal with these Bunyans.
Pat I didn't know you were a chiropodist.
Howard (*picking up a moderately large pile and heading for the door*) And where's bloody Oliver Goldsmith?
Pat I expect his train's late. Or his mother. You know what his mother's like. Oh, Howard ——

Howard carries on moving

Howard?
Howard (*stopping*) Yes?
Pat Are we penalizing spellings?
Howard Such as?
Pat Wordsworth.

Howard As in?
Pat (*looking at the paper she is marking*) William Wordsworth.
Howard As in how spelt?
Pat With two u's.
Howard A mark off each time.
Pat She's done it all the way through.
Howard Tough.
Pat She'll be into minus marks by the end.
Howard It's a set text, Pat. This is A level. If she can't spell the author's name after two years ...
Pat It's such a shame. She's got lovely handwriting.
Howard I've got to go ... If you see Boswell...
Pat Oh, Howard ...
Howard What? What?
Pat We need to have a little talk.
Howard Not now, Pat. I can't have a little talk now, for God's sake ...

There is a bleeping noise; Howard's pager has gone off in his pocket

That's my pager. My pager's gone off.
Pat Not now. I didn't mean now. I meant sometime.
Howard Sometime. Fine. (*He wiggles his pocket at Pat*) Will you see please what number's on my pager?
Pat (*rummaging in Howard's pocket, finding the pager and reading*) 01932 ——
Howard Oh, Byfleet. Now what?
Pat Sometime this weekend, then?
Howard Sometime. Yes.

Howard leaves, rapidly, slamming the door

After a few moments, the door creaks open slowly again. Pat looks at it, sighs, goes over, closes it and returns to her papers

The door L flies open. It is Ian. He carries a massive pile of papers

Ian Where's Johnson?
Pat Johnson?
Ian Howard.
Pat Just this minute gone.
Ian Was he looking for Boswell?

Pat bursts out laughing

What?

Pat I thought it was — I thought you were — Johnson looking for his Boswell. You see?

Ian (*puzzled*) No.

Pat Samuel Johnson and his biographer, something — I can't remember — Boswell.

Ian Haven't read them.

Pat And we've got Howard Johnson and Terry Boswell. After all these years I've only just made the connection.

Ian So he was looking for Boswell?

Pat Who?

Ian Howard.

Pat I think so.

Ian Because Boswell's looking for him. Was he holding an armful of Dickens?

Pat Boswell?

Ian Johnson.

Pat An armful of Bunyans.

Ian Bunyans? Christ! Boswell's just given me all these!

Pat What are those?

Ian *Lost.*

Pat So he found them?

Ian Who?

Pat Boswell.

Ian What?

Pat You said they were lost.

Ian *Paradise Lost.* Bloody Milton. Miserable streak of English puritan piss. Boswell says we're to mark this lot. No way. No bloody way. He gets a titchy wee pile of Smolletts and dumps this festering great mound on us. I've got to tell Johnson. *Paradise Lost.* (*He laughs grimly*) Bloody apt for this place, eh?

Ian, still carrying the papers, goes out of the door R, *doing the foot trick to slam the door*

After a few seconds the door creaks open again. Pat looks at it, sighs, goes over and closes it. She returns to her papers and her marking

The door L *flies open and Howard rushes in with a huge pile of papers*

Howard Have you seen Ian?

Pat Just this minute gone.

Howard Was he looking for me?

Pat Yes.

Howard puts the huge pile of papers down on another table

Howard *Godots.* Did he have an armful of Miltons?
Pat Godot?
Howard Ian.
Pat Think so.
Howard Well he shouldn't have! What the hell was he doing with those? I'm going to have this out with Boswell.
Pat Don't shout at me! It's not my fault!
Howard Which way did he go?

Pat indicates the door R

I like that, by the way.
Pat What?
Howard What you're wearing. On a scale of ten it's a definite eight. You always look good in green.

Pat looks at what she is wearing in a puzzled way. It is pink

Howard goes, slamming the door

Pat Green? (*She glares at the door*)

As if by Pat's will power only, the door stays shut. Pat turns back to her pile of marking

The door R bursts open again and Howard enters

Howard I forgot. I'm going to need the data from the marked pilot samples at the team meeting. Can you tell everyone? Pat?
Pat Yes.
Howard Right.
Pat Howard, when exactly can we have this chat of ours. Because I've got something I desperately ——
Howard That isn't your marked pilot sample, is it?
Pat Unmarked, mostly. Actually. Strictly speaking.
Howard Strictly speaking, Pat, that should have been done before you came.
Pat Not possible, Howard.
Howard Team meeting in five minutes. Tell everyone. And where's Oliver-bloody-Goldsmith?
Pat Howard, our chat ——

Howard's pager goes off again

Howard Get thee behind me, Byfleet …

Howard exits, slamming the door

Pat And it's not green! (*She stares at the door* R *again and eventually averts her eyes*)

The door R *creaks slowly open. Pat closes it, sighs and settles back to her pile*

After a few moments the door L *opens and Judith pokes her head through. She has her raincoat on and is carrying an overhead projection machine*

Judith Excuse me…
Pat (*fiercely*) Yes?
Judith Is this Team B?
Pat No.
Judith Oh. Right. Sorry to disturb.

Judith exits, puzzled, shutting the door

Pat Or are we? Oh God, I think we are … (*She runs over to the door* L)

The door creaks slowly open as Pat approaches it. She stops in her tracks for a moment, shakes her head and peers round the door

Hallo? Sorry … Yes, this is … Oh.

There is obviously nobody there. She comes back into the room, closes the door and returns to her marking

After a few moments the door creaks open again to reveal Oliver, who obviously has something on the floor outside because he takes a step out of view, bending over

On hearing the door open, Pat closes her eyes in desperation, so she doesn't see Oliver. She moves quickly across to the door and grabs it. The audience sees, but Pat doesn't, that Oliver straightens up, holding a briefcase and what is obviously a very heavy overhead projection machine. Pat closes the door with a wholly exaggerated care and stomps back to her desk. There is a pause. The door creaks slowly open to reveal Oliver standing there again, minus machine. He bends out of view to pick it up. Pat flies across the room and slams the door viciously, just as Oliver appears holding the machine once more. There is a loud crash from outside the door. Pat storms back to her table, muttering. There is a pause. Then a muffled tap at the door. Pat closes her eyes and tries to ignore it. There is another, slightly louder knock. Pat flies across to the door and flings it open

(*Screaming*) Yes? What is it? For God's sake, I am trying to mark in here!
Oliver Ah, hallo, Pat.
Pat Oh. Oliver! I'm so sorry. I didn't realize.
Oliver Quite all right, quite all right.
Pat Come in, let me help you with ——
Oliver No, no, I've got it balanced nicely now. I think if I just … (*He puts the machine on a table with much obvious relief and puts his briefcase by the hatstand*)
Pat I'm so sorry, Oliver, it's been like the M25 in here this morning …
Oliver I shouldn't be lifting heavy weights. Not with my problematic back.
(*He takes his coat off during the following*)
Pat Why on earth were you?
Oliver Johnson.
Pat Oh.
Oliver That Johnson — person. He's the absolute ruddy limit. I'm sorry, Pat.
I apologize for my language, but he really is insufferable.
Pat He's under a lot of ——
Oliver No, honestly. Really. I've only just arrived here, you see? Very well,
I admit I was a teeny bit late, but can I help it if my connecting train pulls
out seven seconds early? Seven seconds. I'm sure they did it on purpose.
They could see me running up the concourse, waving. So I paid for a taxi
all the way here ——
Pat Oh dear.
Oliver — so as not to be mortifyingly late ——
Pat You shouldn't have done that.
Oliver (*putting his coat back on again*) — and the first person I bump into
is him. The Johnson man. Howard. I haven't seen him for a year, a whole
year. Not since last year, in fact, this time last year. Does he say hallo? No.
Does he ask after my health? Mother's? No. "Where have you been?" His
first words. And doesn't give me a chance to justify myself. Oh no. "We
need that upstairs," he says, pointing. And marches off.
Pat You had to carry that all the way upstairs? You shouldn't have had to
do that ——
Oliver It's the same every year. Every year.
Pat — not with your back.
Oliver He's got it in for me. That's the long and the short of it. It's a horrible
phrase, most infelicitous, but it's true. He has got it in for me.

The door flies open and Howard enters, carrying a huge pile of papers

Howard You not staying, Oliver?
Oliver What?
Howard Coat.
Oliver I ——

Howard Team meeting. Don't forget. In here. Five minutes. Don't wander off.

Howard goes, pulling the door to behind him with his foot

Oliver stands there, fuming. There is an awkward pause

Pat How is your mother, Oliver?
Oliver Insufferable. Absolutely insufferable.
Pat Oh dear. I am sorry. She's got worse, then?
Oliver (*taking his coat off and hanging it up*) Mmm? No, not Mother. Him. Johnson. I might as well be invisible. I might as well be a dog. I ... Sorry, Patricia. I'm so sorry. My *bête noire*, I'm afraid. Mother? Yes, Mother. Oh she's ... You know. Well, insufferable, actually.
Pat Oh dear.
Oliver No, no. I'm being unfair. She doesn't get any worse.
Pat Good. That's good.
Oliver She doesn't get any better, either, come to that. She's eighty-four, you know.
Pat Goodness. Well, yes, she would be. She was eighty-three last year.
Oliver Yes, yes. Of course, there was the usual fuss about me coming here this weekend. The usual scenes. She really can be ... She accused me of dumping her simply so that I could swan off and enjoy myself. She has a very strange idea of what happens at these weekends. She certainly hasn't met Johnson. But it's the usual strategy. She hasn't spoken to me at all since a week last Monday. Not even about the bedpan incident. And she was sick four times on the ferry, which is no mean achievement on a twenty minute crossing in calm weather from Ryde to Portsmouth.
Pat Oh dear.
Oliver Still, at least she didn't lock herself in the life-jacket cupboard and refuse to come out after we reached the mainland.
Pat That's an improvement on last year, anyway.
Oliver Happy days.
Pat And she's staying with her friend again, is she?
Oliver Near the harbour, yes. It's very convenient. And she nearly always calms down once she gets to Lavinia's and she can get her dentures out. She doesn't seem to want me at all once she's there. I crept away and left them over a cup of tea, gumming away at each other, nineteen to the dozen.
Pat Lovely.
Oliver I gather we've a new member of the team this year?
Pat Oh God. That was her.
Oliver Whom?
Pat The girl who thought this was Team B but I told her it wasn't, when it is, of course, but — it doesn't matter.

Oliver How's your husband? Gordon.
Pat Gareth. Fine.
Oliver And those two strapping boys of yours?
Pat Three. They're fine.
Oliver Good. Good.

Ian enters. He is waving a single sheet of paper

Ian Anyone seen the Pope?
Oliver Ah, Ian, young fellow me lad! How are you?
Ian I'm looking for the Pope.
Oliver Well, he's usually to be seen standing on a balcony, banning prophylactics in Latin.
Ian Alexander Pope.
Oliver Ah. Dead, I believe. Sorry.
Ian I found a Pope at the bottom of a pile of Bunyans. Who's marking the Pope?
Oliver Somebody from the Protestant back four?
Ian You what?
Oliver Footer. Come on, old boy, you're a Scottie. Keep up.
Ian I hate football.
Pat Try Terry Boswell.
Oliver Ah yes. He's a great Augustan. Or so he likes to think.
Ian Terry Boswell. Right. Honest ——
Oliver (*under his breath*) Honestly…
Ian — this whole place is in chaos.
Oliver No, no, Ian. Now there you are mistaken. The computer at Byfleet is, in fact, making us very much more efficient. I know this for a fact because Howard told me. It has, apparently, rationalized the whole process and made us more efficient. I was grateful for the information, because to these untutored eyes it does, as you say, my dear young fellow, look very much like chaos.
Ian The computer at Byfleet's gone down.
Oliver I've no idea what that means, but I'm sure it's no less than it deserves.
Ian I've got to find Terry Boswell.
Oliver Team meeting in five minutes, Ian.
Ian Right.

Ian exits, doing the foot and the door trick

Oliver About the same time the flying pigs come in for their landing.

Pat returns to her rather frantic marking

I say — surely that isn't your marked pilot sample, Patricia?
Pat Yes, it is.
Oliver Oh, but surely those were supposed to be marked by ——
Pat That's right, Oliver. I know.
Oliver (*tutting*) They should have been marked before we arrived.
Pat I know that. I had a few — distractions.
Oliver I finished mine off last week.
Pat Jolly good.
Oliver I like to get things done in plenty of time. Gave them a last check on the ferry. They were abominable, of course. It goes without saying.

Pat mouths Oliver's next two lines. She has heard it all for many years

The standard slips every year. Change and decay in all around I see. Is there anything I can do, Patricia? To help speed things up?
Pat Perhaps if you could just put the ones I've marked into alphabetical order that might save some time later?
Oliver Of course, of course. This pile? (*He indicates the huge pile*)
Pat This one. (*She indicates the small pile*)
Oliver (*surprised and a bit shocked*) This one? Oh, Patricia, you don't mean to say ——
Pat Please, I know. It seems to take me forever, I don't know why. Please, just don't say anything.
Oliver I'm going to get you a nice cup of tea from the tea rooms when I've done this. That's what's called for. A nice cup of tea and a Danish pastry. Alphabetical order?

Pat nods

Now then, let me see … (*He sorts through the pile*) Ackland, Zuckerman, Smith. Hmm. Quite a challenge. Now — yes, I think I've got the hang of it — there! All done. (*He picks up the last sheet of paper and looks at it*) Ttt, ttt. Dear, oh dear. Wordsworth with two u's. I don't know. Tch, tch. Poor old William.

The door opens and Judith staggers in, holding her overhead projector

Judith This is Team B.
Pat Yes. Oh, I'm sorry, I didn't ——
Judith Is this for in here?
Oliver In point of fact, we have one already.
Judith Well now you've got two. Howard Johnson told me to bring it.
Oliver We'll be seeing double.

Judith Where do you want this? Because actually I don't think I can stand around holding this for much longer.

Oliver Oh please, allow me …

Pat Your back, Oliver.

Judith Just tell me where to put it. That'll be fine.

Oliver Oh well, near a power point, I should think, wouldn't you, Patricia?

Pat Oh, don't ask me. You know me and high-tech.

Judith Here then.

Oliver Well — perhaps here would be …

Judith Here.

Oliver Yes. There will be ——

Judith plonks the projector down on a table with a crash

Whoops. I believe they're quite delicate, these things.

Judith Are they? Thanks for telling me.

Oliver Oh yes. Chock-a-block with delicate mechanisms, all of them designed to make our lives immeasureably easier. Nature spends billions of years and all her largesse manufacturing chalk, but, no, man has to invent a machine to improve upon it. Hallo. Oliver Goldsmith, no relation …

Judith *(ignoring this)* Judith Singeissen. No relation to what?

Oliver *(under his breath)* To whom. *(To Judith)* Oliver Goldsmith, the eighteenth-century playwright.

Judith Why would I think you'd be a relation?

Oliver May I introduce Patricia Cunningham?

Judith We've met before.

Pat It's Pat. Sorry about all the confusion earlier.

Judith No problem.

Pat If you'll excuse me I have to get back to ——

Judith Is that your marked profile sample? I thought that was supposed to ——

Oliver *(jumping in)* Well, Judith, welcome to our happy little band of examiners.

Judith Thanks.

Oliver You'll find that we're much the same as any other hierarchical institutionalized power structure. In other words, we're riven by petty rivalries, flayed by naked ambition and exhibit a slavish adherence to whatever the latest fashionable gobbledegook happens to be. I believe that this year it's modular cross-referencing, or some such nonsense, is it not, Patricia?

Judith Actually that's my field.

Oliver Your field?

Judith It's why I've been brought on to the team. I helped to write the new modular syllabus.

Oliver Really? How interesting. Now let me tell you about our little empire.
There's God, in the form of Gerald Spinks, the Chief Examiner ——
Pat Soon to be *retired* Chief Examiner ——
Oliver Indeed. And then there are his two archangels, though never was a
term more inaccurately used. Both, of course, vying for God's place when
he ceases to exist. They are Terence Boswell, leader of Team A, and
Howard Johnson, leader of Team B. Boswell and Johnson they may be, but
Boswell and Johnson they are most decidedly are not, if you follow me. (*He
laughs*)

Judith smiles thinly

> Of Terence Boswell, or Terry, as I believe he likes to be known — no doubt
> soon to be even further shortened to Tel or Tel Boy, or something equally
> ghastly — I know very little save that he is given to wearing tracksuits at
> breakfast. Of Howard Johnson: well, what shall I say of Howard Johnson,
> our noble leader?

Pat suddenly looks up. She has remembered something

Pat Oliver...
Oliver He is the epitome of energy misdirected. He is the supreme pontiff
of self-serving hypocrisy. He is the *nonpareil* of aggressive rudeness and
arrogance. And I firmly believe he has rampant halitosis, though I try not
to get close enough to confirm this empirically.
Pat (*trying to sugar the pill*) Don't you teach with Howard, Judith?
Judith Yes.
Pat Isn't that a coincidence, Oliver?
Oliver Yes, isn't it?
Judith I'm his second in the department.
Oliver Really? There is a thing. This is in the comprehensive?
Judith Yes.
Oliver Oh.
Judith Meaning what?
Pat Oliver's grant-maintained.
Oliver (*to Pat*) You might have told me, Patricia.
Pat Only just remembered, Oliver.
Oliver Where was I? Oh yes. Then there's young Ian. Wee Ian. The Rob Roy
of the red pen. You don't work with Ian?

Judith shakes her head

> What does one say about Ian? Did I tell you, Patricia? I bumped into him
> downstairs. Dear, dear.

Ian enters, unobserved by Oliver. He carries a huge pile of papers

Pat (*hissing*) Oliver…

Oliver He has string in his shoes again this year. In lieu of shoelaces. You'd think that young wife of his would see that he was properly turned out for these occasions. A proper haircut, a decent shave. Shoelaces. I mean, a pony-tail and string. If we cannot set proper standards how can we expect our students to ——

Ian very deliberately slams the door

He's standing behind me isn't he?

Ian (*whispering murderously into Oliver's ear*) I like string. (*He heads for the door — not the one he entered through*)

Oliver Quite so. Jolly useful stuff. I'm never without it myself. (*To Judith, trying to make amends*) No, he's an awfully nice chap, Ian. Awfully nice. Very sweet nature, you'll find.

Ian tries to open and close the door with his foot, but the string in his shoes becomes entangled and the weight of the papers makes him topple over once he is off balance. He crashes to the floor and the papers fly everywhere

Ian Oh, shite! Fuck, fuck, fuck and double fucking shite!

There is an embarrassed silence. Ian goes down on his hands and knees to reassemble the mass of papers

Oliver (*clearing his throat*) No, no you'll be all right, once you get the hang of the ropes.

Pat (*laughing weakly*) Or the string.

Judith Do you think so?

Oliver Oh yes. What we're doing this morning, you see, is to compare our sample marks. That's the mark that we've all already done — well, most of us have done — prior to arriving here.

Judith Yes, I ——

Oliver Now, you see, we've all marked the same cross-section of essays, by the same sample of candidates, on each A level set text.

Judith Yes, I have actually ——

Oliver And, having compared marks, discussed their relative virtues and failings — of which there are many this year — and got an idea of standards, this afternoon we go to a larger meeting with the whole consortium to thrash out a mutually agreed marking scheme. Because the rest of the consortium's been huddled away in rooms like this all over this lovely old house, marking and grading away, just like us.

Pat It conjures up an odd picture, doesn't it? Lots of different little groups of people, all working away marking the same bits of paper and then shuffling them around for other people to pore over ... I always think it's very ——

Ian pops up from behind the sofa

Ian Orwellian?
Pat No, the German man...
Ian Kafka?
Pat Yes.
Judith Czech.
Pat You'd thought of it, too?
Judith Kafka was Czech.
Ian Was he? I didn't know that. Haven't read him.

Ian disappears behind the sofa

Oliver Anyway, then, and only then, we get down to marking the allotted in-depth sampling of our assigned questions, to wit ——
Judith Shakespeare, Wordsworth and Dickens.
Oliver You know?
Judith I have actually done it before. For another board.
Oliver Oh. Another board?
Judith The Northern Board.
Oliver (*dubiously*) Oh. The *Northern* Board. Oh well — I think you'll find we're something else altogether.
Judith Yes. I'm beginning to realize that.
Oliver Good, good. We'll soon have her broken in, won't we, young Ian?
Ian Undoubtedly.
Oliver Ian will soon lick you into shape.

Howard staggers in, stepping over Ian with his arms once more full of papers

Howard Not the most convenient of places, actually, Ian.
Ian Sorry.
Howard What are those?
Ian Hardy. *Return of the* bloody *Native*.
Howard They're for Terry Boswell.
Ian He says not.
Howard They bloody well are.
Oliver Or Howard. Now Howard will lick you into shape.
Howard Sorry for the delay. Can we make a start on the cross-referencing pilot sample meeting?

Pat (*marking furiously*) Just a minute, just a minute …

Howard Terry Boswell's team have already apparently finished their sample mark, I don't know when — in between their game of football and session in the bar, I suppose — so if we don't get under way soon …

Ian (*indicating the pile that Howard has brought in*) What are these?

Howard Oh. Those. I'll come to those in a moment.

Oliver puts up his hand

Is this going to be one of your points of order, Oliver, because if it is, frankly I don't think we have the time …

Oliver gives a significant look to Pat but points at Judith

Oh yes. Can I introduce a new face this year ——?

Oliver Thank you, Oliver …

Howard What?

Oliver Nothing. Nothing at all.

Howard And a very welcome one, needless to say. She comes highly recommended by none other than Gerald Spinks himself, and I'm sure she's going to become a valued and trusted colleague. Judith, this is Ian. Pat. Oliver. Two of our old stalwarts.

Oliver I think I object to stalwarts, Howard. Do you think we should object to stalwarts, Patricia?

But Pat is marking too furiously to notice

It makes me feel like an old and rather rusty battleship.

Ian wanders across to look at the pile of papers that Howard brought in earlier

Ian Hang on, hang on!

Howard Ian …

Ian These are the *Paradise Lost* scripts.

Howard Yes, that's right, I ——

Ian Poxy bloody Milton. I gave these back to Terry Boswell!

Howard Yes, you did, and ...

Ian And what? Because I'm not marking the bloody things, I can tell you that for ——

Howard Now just a moment, Ian, I'm team leader and after considerable negotiation with Terry Boswell it's been decided that Team B ——

Ian Us.

Howard Us, yes, if you want to put it that way. That we should be responsible for *Paradise Lost*.

Oliver Oh, now, just a moment ...

Ian So we're not only doing the Shakespeare and the Dickens, the Wordsworths, the Miltons and all?

Oliver (*under his breath*) As well.

Ian And Terry Boswell says we're doing the Hardys?

Howard That's up for negotiation.

Ian So were the Miltons and look what happened!

Pat And we're still waiting for *Godot*.

Howard Gerald Spinks is arbitrating on that, as you know, Pat.

Ian Ay, and I think we've a pretty shrewd idea which way it'll go. Because this is all about you toadying up to Gerald bloody Spinks, isn't it, eh?

Howard I resent that.

Oliver That does mean an enormous number of scripts.

Howard We're only doing the cross-sectional referencing mark, Oliver.

Ian That's a hundred scripts of each author!

Oliver You said you negotiated this. What did Terry Boswell's team get in return?

Howard It's all fair. They've got the Pope.

Ian That's twenty-five scripts, max.

Howard The Smolletts.

Ian Only about five kids were stupid enough to do that old windbag.

Howard And the *Golden Poets Of The Silver Age*.

Oliver How many of those?

Howard I've really no idea.

Judith I marked that last year — admittedly it was only for the *Northern* Board — but it was thirteen scripts and one spoiled paper covered in the candidate's regurgitated breakfast.

Ian Jesus.

Howard Now, Ian ——

Ian That's what it is, isn't it? Creeping up to Gerald Spinks so's you'll get the Chief Examinership. Waving your willy; "Look Gerald, mine's bigger than Terry Boswell's!"

Oliver Oh, I say, now, Ian, ladies present ...

Ian Well, what else is it? Either that or Terry Boswell's run rings round you 'cos you're too stupid to ...

Howard I resent all this.

Ian Or you're frightened of him. Is that it? Well, I'm not frightened of him. I'm going down there to the Library to tell him where he can stuff his Miltons. And you might like to wonder, folks, why Terry Boswell's team get to work in all that space in the Library and we get cooped up in here. I'm off.

Howard You stay where you are, Ian. I'm telling you.

Ian moves to the door with a snort

Judith (*wandering across to the* Godot *pile*) Are these the Hardys? Right. Ian, you take the *Paradise Lost*s. I'll bring these. (*She picks up the* Godot *pile*)

Ian takes the Paradise Lost *papers and goes out*

Judith walks to the door

Howard Now wait a minute — where are you going?
Judith To see Terry Boswell. Somebody's got to do something before everything goes to hell.
Oliver (*laughing*) Oh. Very apt!
Judith Is it?
Oliver *Paradise Lost* — goes to hell. Do you see?

Judith goes out

Howard sinks down with his head in his hands. Pat and Oliver stand awkwardly

(*Eventually*) Well, time for that tea and Danish pastries, I think. Yes, tea and Danish pastries are definitely called for. Patricia?

Pat shakes her head

Howard?

No response

Right.

Oliver exits

There is a long pause. Eventually Howard lets out a huge frustrated sigh. Pat looks at him

Pat Oh, Howard …

And, unable to hold back any longer, Pat rushes across to Howard and cradles him in her arms

Howard! My poor darling! My poor, poor darling!

Howard's sigh turns into a howl and he snuggles into Pat

There, there. There, there — ssssh ...

Howard I do my best, Pat ——

Pat I know, I know ...

Howard — but sometimes I just feel so ——

Pat Unvalued. I know — sssh — ssh ...

Howard Everybody just thinks I do all this because I'm career oriented ——

Pat Sssh ... no they don't, no they don't ...

Howard — but nobody comes into education if they're really ambitious. Not really. I do it because I care, Pat. I really care. Imparting knowledge to young minds. That's what turns me on. The sight of a young face, eager for knowledge. Experience. All that sort of thing.

Pat I know, sweetheart. I know.

Howard Bloody Terry Boswell.

Pat Let it out, my love. Let it out.

Howard Terry Boswell with his Oxford accent and his fake bloody tan and white teeth. If you want to see the face of somebody who's just in this for the power, you look into those cold blue eyes, Pat. When you look into those cold blue eyes — they mesmerize you. You just stand there and nod. He refused point blank, you know, to take those Miltons. Point blank. What could I say? All of Team A standing behind him, grinning. That's the difference, you see? He's got his team behind him. Four square. All of them. Not like ... Well, he hasn't got bloody bolshy Ian to contend with. Bloody insidious Oliver. He's got solidarity. But me, I'm vulnerable, do you see? I'm vulnerable on all counts.

Pat I love your vulnerability.

Howard Nobody else sees it, Pat. I don't show it to anybody else. Nobody apart from you.

Pat Oh, Howard. My love.

They sit for a long moment

Howard — I think this might be the moment for our little chat.

Howard Hmmm?

Pat I've decided to leave.

Howard Hmmm?

Pat To leave. Gareth ...and the boys.

Howard Gareth?

Pat My husband.

Howard (*looking ashen but managing to assume a rather false enthusiasm*) Are you sure that … I mean, that's wonderful. God, wonderful — but are you sure it's the right thing to do'?

Pat It's been the hardest decision I've ever had to make. But there's nothing there for me.

Howard What … ? Not even — the children?

Pat The boys …

Howard Boys, yes.

Pat I never see them, Howard. Gareth makes sure of that. Where are they this weekend? Off climbing Snowdon or some bloody mountain. And if it's not mountaineering it's orienteering. And if it's not orienteering it's cycling or windsurfing or EuroDisney or shark fishing.

Howard He — keeps them pretty busy then?

Pat So I never see them at weekends. And then, of course, in the week it's squash or fencing every evening. Country dancing. Can you believe that? He takes them country fucking dancing on a Wednesday.

Howard Can't you tag along?

Pat Gareth says they're not women's pursuits.

Howard Country dancing?

Pat He says I've got two left feet. I'd only clutter things up. Get in the way. Of all this male bonding presumably. That's what he says.

Howard Of course …

Pat What?

Howard You've been away for quite a lot of weekends yourself.

Pat What do you mean?

Howard Courses and suchlike.

Pat What — you mean the courses we go on?

Howard Yes.

Pat I go on those courses so we can be together.

Howard Yes, of course.

Pat We go on those courses so we can be together! Those are the only times we can be together!

Howard Yes, yes. I know!

Pat Hundreds and hundreds of courses! My Headteacher's getting bloody suspicious, do you know that? He stops me every Friday afternoon and asks me what course I'm on this weekend and jokes about me bankrupting the school.

Howard You're exaggerating.

Pat The only reason I do this bloody marking is so we can come on this weekend and be together!

Howard I know, I know!

Pat Do you think I'd have submitted myself to this — this torture — for seven years if … Well what do you think I've done it for? The money? Do you think I'd have put up with this just for the money? Gareth earns the money!

Gareth earns more money than we know what to do with, so do you think
I'd do this if it'd been just for the money?

Howard No, no. I know!

Pat I hate marking! Marking makes me ill, I worry about it so much, the effect
my terrible marking could be having on these young peoples' lives, their
futures! But I do it for you! For us! Do you think I've put up with all these
years rolling round on the beds made for anorexic dwarfs they have in these
places — do you think I've put up with that because I enjoy it?

Howard Oh, thanks very much.

Pat Well, I have enjoyed it, of course I've enjoyed it. I love it. I love that. With
you. Wherever it happens.

Howard Then why are you getting in a state like this?

Pat Because I don't understand what point you were trying to make.

Howard All I meant was — that it might not all be one-sided. It might not
all be Gareth taking the boys away because you've not been there when
you've been — with me on — courses. All I'm saying is, it might all be
chicken, egg. Egg, chicken.

Pat What are you talking about, Howard?

Howard Six of one and half a dozen of the other. Which came first? You or
Gareth? Do you see?

Pat Do you think I started all this lightly? Seven years ago? Do you think I
just did it for a bit of fun? Do you not think that there was something
lacking, something seriously lacking in my marriage for me to start this in
the first place? Do you not think that I found something with you that I
couldn't find anywhere else? And that's why I've put up with rolling
around in a two-foot wide bed with springs sticking out. But now I'm
saying we can be rid of all that. We can be together. We can live in a house
and sleep together in a double bed. We can be a proper couple.

There is a long silence. Howard's face stiffens and he doesn't look at Pat

(*Eventually; turning away*) Oh fine.

Howard stands up, walks stiffly to the door R *and goes out*

*After a few moments the door creaks slowly open. Oliver is behind it,
holding a cup of tea, on top of which is balanced a plate with a Danish
pastry on it*

*With a cry of animal rage Pat screams towards the door, slams it with an
almighty bang and goes back to her table. The door slowly swings open to
reveal Oliver standing amidst the wreckage of his tea*

Oh … oh … Oliver. What can I say? (*She offers to help him*) Here…

Oliver No, don't worry. Really. You know what they say — one door closes and another one opens. That only seems to be half true today.

Pat Let me help you get ——

Oliver One should count one's blessings in small things: I think the Danish pastry's survived intact.

Pat Your lovely suit.

Oliver Just an old thing. My father's actually. I've never really grown into it. I say, I just saw Johnson in the corridor. Our Howard.

Pat Oh yes?

Oliver He looked terribly upset.

Pat Did he?

Oliver (*beaming*) Yes, he did. As I say, one finds one's comforts in the small things.

Pat He's ——

Oliver What?

Pat Nothing. It's just that he's under the most enormous pressure. You must appreciate that.

Oliver Nonsense.

Pat Oliver, please …

Oliver Who puts him under all this supposed pressure? Nobody but himself! He's got everything in life a man could ask for. A beautiful, talented wife, a gorgeous, Edwardian house, charming clutch of identical twin girls. And what does he do? He puts it all in jeopardy.

Pat (*guiltily*) What do you mean?

Oliver By running himself ragged, dashing around trying to seem important. Do you know, he's got about four jobs all told? I gather he's Head of Department, Head of Pastoral Care and directs all the school plays himself. On top of all that he does private tuition and goes in for all of this examining business in his spare time. And, of course, he's desperate to take over Gerald Spinks' job. Why, in God's name? Why?

Pat Oh, I don't know, Oliver. I really don't. Perhaps there's a void in his life.

Oliver Rubbish.

Pat He obviously finds something here that doesn't exist in other parts of his ——

Oliver Utter rubbish. Have you met his wife?

Pat No.

Oliver I have. Elspeth. She's a very beautiful woman. Very. Ethereal. Sensitive. Talented. A first rate harpist.

Pat She sounds lovely. (*She finds it very hard to control herself during the following*)

Oliver Why a man wants to spend his weekends away from such a woman I can't begin to imagine. But his relentless ambition has taken its toll on her as well, do you see? She's been in and out of nursing homes over the years. Nervous trouble. Well, we all know what that means. And we don't have to look too far for the cause. I tried to tell him once. Out of my concern, out of the goodness of my heart. He told me to mind my own expletive deleted business. (*Pause*) I've just had an idea. Perhaps you could have a word with him? Put him back on the right track? He might listen to a more mature woman.

Pat breaks down

Pat? Is everything... ? What's the — look, please, I know what it is. How insensitive of me. Please — don't worry about the suit! A good sponging down and ... I think it's dry cleanable, so please ...

Judith and Ian enter. Ian is still holding the pile of Paradise Lost *scripts*

Judith What's going on?
Oliver Oh, nothing at all, really. A small incident with a cup of tea and a Danish pastry.

Pat gathers herself together and exits by the other door

Low blood sugar, I think. I'll look after her. A visit to the tea room is called for, I fancy. Soon put her right. Excuse me.

Oliver follows Pat out and slams the door behind him

Ian (*looking at his watch*) Ay, it's round about the time.
Judith What time?
Ian Every year it's the same. You walk into a room somewhere, sometime round about now, and you find Pat in floods and Oliver wall-eyed in blank incomprehension. It's a well-worn ritual.
Judith You mean that Pat and Oliver are having an affair?
Ian Och, God, no! What a stomach-churning thought. No. Her and Howard. Which is nearly as bad, now I come to think of it.
Judith Pat and Howard are having an affair?
Ian It's not an affair, sweetheart! It's an historical saga! It's been going on for years.
Judith But they can hardly ever see each other, surely?
Ian That's why they go on courses. All the time. Or they do things like this. So they can be together. Honest, they're a Staff Development Officer's dream. What they don't know about Classroom Management Techniques, Curriculum Development and Educational Psychology can be written on the back of a Rizla paper. No, it's true! Funny thing is, they think nobody notices, but for a while a couple of years ago it got to be so embarrassingly noticeable that some wit started a Howard and Pat Newsletter. They did.

It used to go the rounds of local staffrooms. You know: "Last spotted enjoying the three days and two sultry nights of the *Coping with the Anorexic Sixth Former* Course at Lancaster, long-time lovers Howard and Pat, dot, dot, dot ..." It was quite popular for a bit.

Judith You're making that up.

Ian I might be. What's he like to work for, old Howard?

Judith (*thinking*) Diverse.

Ian I can imagine. Bet he's a terrible teacher, too, eh?

Judith No comment.

Ian Oh, I see. Ay, well, that'd be right. What did he call you? "A valued colleague".

Judith Is that supposed to have some special meaning?

Ian Not really. It just usually means that he's got it in mind to shag somebody.

Judith Are you going to put those down?

Ian Oh. Ay. (*He puts down the pile of papers*)

Howard comes in. He seems to have collected himself a bit. He smiles a rather bitter but triumphant smile as he sees the pile of papers

Howard No luck with Terry Boswell, then? I could have saved you the journey.

Judith Oh no, it was worth the trip. Very charming man.

Howard Oh yes?

Judith Lovely eyes.

Howard Superficial charm; we've still ended up with the Miltons.

Judith We brokered a deal.

Howard Deal?

Judith We're going to do the *Paradise Lost*s. And Terry's agreed to do the Hardys *and* to tackle those.

Howard The *Godot*s? Well — good. That's good.

Judith He'll send somebody down for them later on.

Ian I still think we'd have been better off marking the *Godot*s. At least it's modern. Bloody *Paradise Lost* ——

Judith Milton's easier to mark.

Ian You're joking. No way.

Judith You don't think so? Then what's *Waiting For Godot* about, Ian? In your opinion?

Ian Well ... eeeh ...

Judith Well?

Ian Ummm. Waiting.

Judith Mmm.

Ian For Godot. And he disnae show up. (*Pause*) And that's about it, really.

Judith And you've got a degree in English.

Ian Comparative Literature, actually.

Judith And if that's all you can come up with, can you imagine the incoherent, half-digested garbage that the average sixth former's going to have poured into this pile of papers? Which makes it hell to mark. Because there are no easy answers. But an essay on *Paradise Lost* — it's a gift for the thickies. They can stick an essay together like an Airfix kit. Good versus evil, Adam and Eve, the Devil gets all the best tunes. An instant essay that's a doddle to mark. Grade E on a good day, near miss on a bad.

Ian Ah, but. But, but, but — (*he flounders*) I don't know what *Waiting For Godot's* on the syllabus for, anyway.

Howard What do you mean?

Ian Because it was originally written in French, wasn't it?

Howard Yes, but Samuel Beckett is, of course, English.

Judith Irish.

Howard Irish. Yes, of course.

Judith And if you take all the Irish authors out of English literature exams, there won't be much left to examine.

Ian Ay, well, I suppose if you put it that way. She's quite clever, really, isn't she?

Howard (*smiling horribly*) And that, Ian, is exactly why I employed her.

Oliver and Pat come in with their cups of tea and cakes

Right, are we all here at last? Then let's make a start on the cross-sectional referencing mark for the full meeting this afternoon. The Tennyson.

Pat rushes across to her table, worried

Pat Oh yes, it's all right. I've finished those.

Oliver Bravo!

Howard Now then, in order to more fully facilitate ——

Oliver groans

—— to facilitate more fully an efficient cross-sectional referencing, I've already spent some considerable time compiling a computer-generated graphical presentation of the matrix grid on several overhead transparencies. (*He flicks the switch on one of the projectors*)

Nothing happens

What's wrong with this?

Pat It's not working.

Howard I can see it's not working.

Oliver I believe the technical term is *gone down*.
Howard Gone down?
Oliver In sympathy with the computer at Byfleet, I expect.
Howard This is nothing like the computer at Byfleet. The bulb's gone. Give
  me a hand, Oliver. We'll use the other one.
Oliver Back. Alas. My back.
Howard Ian.
Ian What? Oh. Right.

Ian and Howard swap the overhead projectors around

Howard Now then. (*He flicks the switch. Nothing happens. He flicks the
  switch uselessly for several seconds*)

*Drily, Oliver reaches into his pocket and produces a stick of chalk, which he
offers to Howard*

Oliver Chalk?
Howard Why didn't somebody check this? Somebody could easily have
  checked this while I was … Do I have to do everything myself?
Judith It's not plugged in.

*Howard seems about to disagree with her but sees that she is right. He plugs
in the machine*

Howard Ian. You operate for me.

Ian picks up the transparencies

  Now, if you could just concentrate your attention on the screen, I'll whisk
  you through the matrix grid to give you the idea. The first transparency's
  just the title page. Transparency one… (*He clicks his fingers*)

*Ian puts on the first transparency. Howard smiles, pleased with his work, and
seems in no hurry to move on until everybody has made approving noises. It
is computer-generated, very impressive*

  (*Nodding, pleased*) Yes, I think you'll find all of this a great help. (*He clicks
  his fingers*)

*Ian replaces the first transparency with the second. The new transparency
has obviously been got at by small children, because Howard's careful work
has been scrawled over in large, childish handwriting done in brightly
coloured pen. It reads:*

"DADDY. WE LOVE YOU. WE WANT TO PLAY WITH YOU.
WHY ARE YOU ALWAYS TOO BUSY TO PLAY WITH US?"
The members of the team look on, appalled but fascinated. Now confident,
Howard does not look at the screen, but looks at his audience and talks

Yes, I think you can see that we'll be able to take an overview of the
situation, using the cross-path analysis function available to us in this
format. (*He clicks his fingers*)

Ian puts up the next transparency. It reads:
"DADDY WHY DO YOU GO AWAY EVERY WEEKEND
WHEN WE WANT TO PLAY WITH YOU? MUMMY CRYS
AND SAYS SHE IS LONELY TOO."

Everyone clear on that one?

The team members nod, mesmerized

Good. (*He clicks his fingers*)

Ian changes the transparency. The next one reads:
"WE HATE YOU DADDY 'COS WHEN YOU COME HOME YOU
SHOUT AT MUMMY AND MAKE MUMMY CRY AGAIN. WE THINK
YOU ARE POO. SIGNED DAISY AND CORDELIA."

And I think that one more or less speaks for itself. Any questions?

The team members shake their heads. Pat looks tearful

Impressive stuff, isn't it, I think you'll agree, even though I do say so
myself. (*He catches sight of their expressions*) What? What? (*He glances
at the screen, does a double take and pales. He whisks the transparency off
the projector, switches the projector off and does a rapid check on the rest
of his presentation. There is obviously more of the same. He stands,
uncertain*) They're, um — yes, well, they're gifted children, you know. I
mean, officially. IQs off the scale. And I'm not just saying that because
they're mine, I ——
Oliver " Out of the mouths of babes and sucklings … "
Howard Shut up, Oliver. And Pat, stop snivelling. Well … A little technical
hitch there, so … Right. Can I suggest that I run verbally through the names,
you tell me the grades you've given, we'll hope that we're all in the same
general area and we'll agree an average. Yes?

There is general agreement

Right. Have you got your papers, Oliver?

Oliver No need. I transcribed the relevant information on the ferry. (*He smugly takes a neatly folded sheet of paper out of his wallet and puts on his half-moon reading glasses*)

Ian Well, aren't we the wee creepy of the class?

Oliver Merely being prepared, young Ian. "Train hard, fight easy". Clausewitz.

Ian What's that? A type of German lager?

Howard I'll start, shall I? Aardmann. That's two A's. Japhet. Japhet Aardmann. E. Judith?

Judith D.

Howard Ian?

Ian D.

Howard Oliver?

Oliver E.

Howard Pat?

Pat B.

Howard B?

Pat B.

Howard All right.

Pat Bottom of the band B.

Howard Right. We'll — come back to it. Now — Buckman, Rachel. A.

Judith B.

Ian B.

Oliver C.

Pat F.

Howard F?

Pat F.

Howard Right, we'll come back to that one. Now. Cholic. Kenneth. E.

Judith D.

Ian D.

Oliver F.

Pat A.

Howard Pat...

Pat I'm sorry, that's what I came out with. A.

Howard (*exhaling*) Flint, Hugh. B stroke C.

Judith A stroke B.

Ian A stroke B.

Oliver B stroke C.

Pat E stroke near miss.

Howard Holligum, Holly. A.

Judith A.

Ian A.

Oliver B.
Pat E.
Howard Move on. Humper. Christopher. F.
Judith F.
Ian F.
Oliver U.
Pat B.
Howard Tostevin, Timothy. D.
Judith D.
Ian D.
Oliver D.

Pat wavers

Howard Pat?
Pat A.
Howard A. Right. Zoster. Karlheinz. A.
Judith A.
Ian A.
Oliver A.
Pat I'm sorry, I ——
Howard Just give us your mark, Pat.
Pat F.

There is a silence

Howard Well, this is a total waste of time, isn't it? How are we going to arrive at an average out of this. Are you on a different planet to the rest of us when you're marking, Pat, or what?
Oliver Howard ...
Pat I did what the rest of you did! I followed the rules, I used my professional judgement. I used this assiduously, to the letter... (*She waves her piece of pink paper in the air*)
Howard What's that?
Pat The marking band guidelines.
Oliver On pink paper?
Pat Pink, yes.
Howard Well, that's ... you silly... you should be working from the green sheet.
Pat Green sheet?
Howard We're all working from the green sheet.

The others produce and wave green sheets of paper

Pat I haven't got a green sheet.

Howard I sent them out to everybody in March, with the completely revised marking matrix ...

Pat I've never had a green sheet.

Howard The pink sheet became completely redundant in March.

Pat But I've used it for everything! Hundreds and hundreds of scripts!

Howard They'll all have to be remarked.

Pat But I can't possibly... I ... What am I going to do? What am I going to do?

Howard Well the least you can do, I think, is to apologize to everybody.

Oliver No need for that.

Howard No, I really think that Pat owes you — us — all an apology. Pat?

Pat I'm — sorry. I'm so sorry.

Howard Right. Thank you, Pat. That's better.

Ian Now what do we do?

Howard I'm not quite sure. On a cock-up scale of ten this is a ——

Ian You're the team leader! You're supposed to be able to make decisions like this.

Oliver (*enjoying himself*) He would seem to have a point.

Howard Shut up, Oliver.

Oliver A little preparation. A modicum of foresight. It goes a long way...

Howard (*holding up a large loose leaf book*) I did prepare. I am prepared. "The Compendium of Marking Guidelines." Our Bible. I have followed every procedure in this manual to the letter. I have kept you informed about the many intricate changes in procedure, time and time again I have stressed to everybody in letters, on the phone: keep on top of the current directives! For crying out loud, Pat, don't you *read*?

Ian Howard, mate, she's in a bit of a state, right?

Howard Oh that's all very well, Ian, mate, but we're hours behind Terry Boswell and Team A as it is. I am going to look an absolute idiot at the meeting this afternoon ...

Oliver History does repeat itself after all.

Howard If you don't shut your smug mouth, Oliver, I'm going to ——

Judith Surely this would be best? We reallocate all of Pat's marking equally amongst ourselves. I'll buy Terry Boswell and his team a few drinks in the bar to distract them from the meeting until we're ready. What do we think?

There is a silence

Well?

Oliver It seems a little unfair on those of us who've done everything that was expected of us well before today's ... But no, of course, Pat. My dear. I'm sorry, I'm being ... Of course. It's the only answer.

Ian I think it's brilliant.

Judith Howard?

Howard Yes, I suppose so.

Judith Then can I suggest the redistribution ought to be ——

Howard I'll do the distribution, Judith. Thank you for your constructive suggestion, but I am team leader.

Oliver (*under his breath*) Worse luck …

Judith Right. Fine.

Ian This really bolsters your faith ——

Oliver (*under his breath*) One's faith…

Ian — in the examinations system, doesn't it?

Howard Oh, and you've got a better way of doing things, have you?

Ian Well how about we get hold of all the scripts, go outside and throw them down the stairs? Those that make it to the bottom get A's and we grade the rest accordingly?

Howard Very funny.

Ian It's no more random than what we're about now.

Howard Fascinating though this is, can we please get on, or we'll be in serious danger of being lapped twice by Terry Boswell. So if you'll all hand in your scripts from the cross-sectional referencing and then, when we've remarked Pat's share, I can collate the marks and come up with the average. I'll have to sacrifice my lunch, but there we are.

Oliver (*handing his piece of paper to Howard*) I think you'll find this completely in order. An orderly, prepared mind doesn't need computerized gimmicks.

Howard Not just your mark sheet, Oliver. I want the actual scripts as well.

Oliver The scripts? Oh, very well.

Howard And can we get this place tidied up a bit, while I tell you about the mark reallocation?

Everyone hands in their papers and then they begin to tidy up the piles of scripts into a reasonable semblance of order. Oliver opens his briefcase to look for his. Obviously what he is expecting to find is not there. During the following he makes increasingly desperate attempts to find what he is looking for in all sorts of places around the room

Pat I'm sorry, I'm so sorry to have caused everybody so much trouble.

Howard Right, this is what we do between now and this afternoon. Ian, you're to take the Wordsworths ——

Ian Haven't read it.

Howard Right, so Judith, you take the Wordsworths.

Judith I'd rather take the *Paradise Lost*s.

Howard Then you take the *Lost*s and I'll take the Wordsworths. Ian, you take the Bunyans.

Ian Haven't read it.

Howard What have you bloody well read, Ian? If your degree's in
Comparative Literature you surely must have read *something* so that you
could compare them? All right. Ian, you take the *Curiosity Shop*s, all right?

Ian (*in pain at the thought*) Ohhhh…

Howard Ian, you are not wriggling out of the *Curiosity Shop*. Pat, using the
proper guidelines this time, you take the *All's Well*s.

*Pat blows her nose and nods. Howard points at the pile of papers in the
corner*

What are those?

Judith *Godot*s. We're still waiting.

Pat gives a brave little chuckle

For Terry Boswell to send somebody down.

Howard All right. And Oliver, you take the Swifts and Bunyans. Oliver?
Oliver?

Pat What's the matter, Oliver?

Oliver I can't find them. They're not here.

Howard What?

Oliver My marked scripts. I thought they were in my briefcase, but they seem
to have disappeared.

Ian Dear, oh dear. And after all that preparation. What would Clausewitz say
about this, Oliver?

Oliver I had them on the bus to the ferry. I had them on the ferry. I ——

Howard What, Oliver. What? Come on, we're wasting time.

Oliver I took them out on the ferry. I remember. Just to give them a final
glance over. This was before mother had her turn and locked herself in the
lavatory. (*He stops, suddenly, full of horror*)

Pat What?

Oliver She asked to have a look at them …

Howard And you let her?

Oliver I was simply grateful that she was speaking to me again.

Howard You showed a non-examiner confidential scripts?

Oliver I often do. We have a little giggle over the examination howlers. It's
good for her. She used to be a teacher once herself, you know.

Howard Dear God, how am I going to break this to Gerald?

Oliver Then I went to the snack bar for some tea and a doughnut, and that
was when she wandered off. A little later I found she'd locked herself in
the … She must have taken the scripts in there with her, and in all the fuss
after we docked … Oh, that woman, that evil, malevolent old woman …

Pat She left them behind in the cubicle, Oliver. That's all. She's old.

Ian Could happen to any of us.

Pat You mustn't blame her.

Oliver Blame her? Left them behind? How can you be so naïve? She's kept them! That's what she's done! Or thrown them away! To punish me for leaving her this weekend!

Pat Oh, Oliver, I don't think so...

Oliver You don't know her. You do not know what she is capable of! She's mad. Possessed. She is capable of anything. Absolutely anything.

Howard How could you, Oliver? How could you do this to me?

Pat (*shouting*) Will you think of somebody apart from yourself for even one second! (*In control again; to Oliver, reasonably*) No, they're here, Oliver. Olly. They must be here. Somewhere in one of these bundles or under all this paper. Come on, everybody! Roll your sleeves up! One last look.

Howard But...

Pat (*shouting again*) Shut up, Howard! Everyone, roll up your sleeves and pitch in. Let's break the habit of a lifetime and be a team!

And with varying degrees of enthusiasm they move bundles of scripts, shift paper and generally undo all the tidying up that they had previously achieved. The scene becomes chaotic

The phone rings. Judith searches for the phone and finds it under a pile of papers. She answers it

Judith Oliver. It's for you.

All activity stops and there is an expectant hush. Oliver walks across and takes the phone

Oliver Thank you, Judith. (*Into the phone*) ... Yes, speaking. ... Oh really? No, I ... Yes, I was ... No, I have absolutely no comment to ... Well, that is your prerogative. Goodbye. (*He puts the phone down. A long pause. He is outwardly calm but it is obviously all he can do not to burst into tears*)

Pat Well?

Oliver That was a young lady from an evening newspaper. They have received a telephone call from an old lady who's found a sheaf of valuable A level papers left on the Isle of Wight ferry. She declined to give her name, but could I confirm that I was the careless examiner responsible? She informed me very politely that they will be running the story in this afternoon's late edition.

Pat Oh dear. Oh no.

Howard groans and holds his head in his hands. Judith is very tight-lipped

There is a knock at the door R

Ian opens the door and exits

Oh. Well. Chin up, everybody. "The worst is not; so long as we can say,
'This is the worst'."
Oliver (*faintly*) *King Lear*, Act Four, Scene One.

Ian returns, holding a large pile of papers

Ian Absolutely spot on there, Pat. (*He lifts a wadge of papers from the top
of the pile*) Because just when you thought he'd pissed off forever, it's *The
Return* … (*he throws down the wadge in disgust*) … *of the* bloody *Native*.

General disillusion; groans all round

Black-out

ACT II

The same, around ten-thirty in the evening

The room is again strewn untidily with papers

Howard, in his shirtsleeves, sits marking the last of his papers. Oliver is on the phone, in quite a distraught state. Howard obviously finds the phone call distracting, because he tuts frequently and sighs heavily

Oliver Mother ... Mother ... Please, can we just have a civilized discussion about this? ... There is no need to scream, Mother, no need at all. Mother, will you please stop screaming? ... I don't think you're wicked, of course I don't think you're wicked. ... Yes, I'm going to take you home. ... To the Island, yes, of course. I know how you hate abroad. ... Yes, I understand why you did it. ... No, I'm not blaming you, Mother. ... No, it's not your fault. It was my fault. It was all my fault. As usual. ...

Judith enters. She has changed her clothes for the evening and looks glamorous. She carries a large pile of papers, which she puts down. During the following she sits

Howard looks up

Listen, Mother, I've got to go. Now, I've arranged for a courier to pick up the papers from Lavinia's and to bring them straight here. ... A courier, mother. A courier. ... A ——

Judith Man with a van.

Oliver A man with a van, yes, thank you. A man with a van, Mother. ... No, it's not to take you off to a home in, Mother. I wouldn't do that. How could you think I'd do that? I'm quite hurt you could even think ... For the examination papers, yes, Mother. ... Right. You've got that? ... Good. ... What? That was Judith. ... Judith. A new member of our team. ... No, I'm not going to run off with her and leave you all alone, Mother. ... What? Yes, she's wearing high heels. ... Yes, some make-up, I think. A little. (*He looks at Judith's skirt*) Shortish, yes. ... Yes, I'll lock the door of my room when I go to bed, Mother. I always do. All right? ... No, I can't, Mother. I can't. ... I just can't, there are people here. (*He takes a deep breath*) No, I don't want you to scream again. Very well. (*He takes another deep breath*) I love you, Mummy. I love you lots. ... Sticky kisses, yes. Good-night. Don't let the bedbugs bite. (*He hangs up*)

Judith has an unreadable expression. Howard's shoulders shake with suppressed laughter. Oliver looks at Howard but decides not to pursue the matter

Well, at least she still has the papers, instead of having burned them or thrown them down the lavatory. One should be grateful for small mercies.
Judith Is she having any treatment?
Oliver Whom?
Judith Your mother.
Oliver Oh yes, tablets for everything. For her waterworks, mostly. And — the other end, you know. Old age. It's a terrible thing.
Judith I didn't mean that kind of treatment. I meant — mentally.
Oliver Mentally? What are you implying? Are you talking about some sort of ... You mean ...
Judith I mean psychiatric help.
Oliver I know what you mean. And on what grounds do you presume to suggest my mother needs psychiatric assistance?
Judith I was just ——
Oliver Have you ever met my mother?
Judith No, of course not.
Oliver Then how do you presume to sit there and say what treatment she should or should not be having?
Judith I couldn't help overhearing your phone call.
Oliver That was a private call.
Judith Then you shouldn't have been making it in public.
Howard He shouldn't have been making it at all in here. Some of us are trying to mark.
Oliver When I made the call I didn't know she was going to ——
Judith Start screaming?
Oliver Yes.
Judith Does she scream a lot?
Oliver I really don't begin to see what business it is of yours. Can I remind you that we have only just met?
Judith I'm not saying it's my business, but if she spends a lot of time screaming for no reason *and* steals things as well, then obviously there's something wrong, isn't there?
Oliver There is nothing wrong with my mother!
Judith It's not a stigma, Oliver. It's an illness. Senile dementia, perhaps. Early stages of Parkinson's.

Oliver And you are an expert on this, are you?

Judith Not an expert, no. But my husband's father had very similar symptoms. It was treatable.

Oliver And that qualifies you to diagnose my mother, does it? And now look what you're making me do: I'm beginning sentences with a conjunction.

Judith I'm just trying to get you to see this objectively.

Oliver But I don't want to see it objectively!

Judith Surely you have to stand back from something like this and look at it rationally? Otherwise you can be so close to the thing that everything gets totally out of proportion.

Oliver I've got it precisely in proportion, thank you.

Judith Have you?

Oliver Exactly in proportion.

Howard It's rather like marking, isn't it?

Oliver Oh, don't you start.

Judith It's exactly like marking.

Oliver He couldn't just sit there and bite his tongue, could he? Oh no, he has to chip in his two pennyworth. And what on earth are you talking about, mental illness and marking exam papers being the same thing. And please ignore the fact that I began that sentence with "and". And that one. My God, what are you people doing to me? My grammar and syntax are disintegrating by the moment!

Judith It's exactly the same thing, Oliver. Objectivity and subjectivity. The trouble is, we all get too involved in everything; our whole approach to the candidates' response is necessarily far too subjective.

Oliver My dear girl, personal responses are subjective. Over the years one develops a feel for the good candidate, an instinct for the excellent.

Judith Listen to the kinds of words you're using. Feel. Instinct. What's objective about that?

Oliver What are you advocating? Multiple response questions? Tick boxes? Right answers and wrong answers, feed the lot into the computer at Byfleet and collate the results on a flow chart?

Howard Nobody's advocating that, Oliver.

Oliver Hamlet was (a) a bit muddled up (b) driven demented by his mother with whom he was in love ——

Howard gives Oliver an ironic look

—— please don't look at me like that, Howard, or (c) was a total psychopath with a poetic bent?

Judith What I'm advocating is more emphasis on process, not outcome. More emphasis on developing communication skills ——

Oliver Aaah! That phrase! This is literature! We are dealing with literature!

Judith — communication skills that have some relevance for the real world. Setting performance criteria and range statements. Monitoring students' performance cumulatively, with a large sample of skills and units that will testify to their acquisition of a wide range of key skills and performance targets.

Oliver Is it me, or has she suddenly started talking Japanese? What is she talking about?

Howard Folks ——

Oliver I know the kind of thing you're advocating — though incidentally, the word advocate has connotations of speaking clearly and understandably ——

Howard Oliver ——

Oliver Performance criteria. Range statements. I saw the outline for one of these courses once. One of the "performance criteria " was that the candidate had to achieve, quote, "An appropriate response to humour." By which they meant laughter, of course, but they couldn't put it that way because then it wouldn't sound utterly mirthless and there might be a danger of somebody actually understanding what they were getting at. I said to Mrs Prendergast in the office, I said, you watch, they'll be having me standing in front of a class reading out jokes from *The Beano* and ticking off a box when they giggle. The whole thing's absurd.

Howard I think you'll find it'd be *Viz*.

Oliver What is?

Howard That you'd have to use nowadays. Not *The Beano* .

Oliver I have no idea what you're talking about. What I'm saying is that it has nothing to do with literature! Great literature! We have nothing to do with it any longer! Once, when we used to come here to sift through the products of young peoples' minds, we used to have a shared ideal. We used to sit out on the lawns here and in between the marking we actually used to talk about literature. You remember that, Howard?

Howard Not sure I do, actually.

Oliver We actually used to *talk* to each other, to exchange thoughts, to share our joy in books and ideas! Now it's all schedules and cross-sectional referencing and critical path analysis. Where is the love of our great English literature in that?

Howard Of course, objectively, it helps if you don't leave the papers you're responsible for marking on the ferry.

There is a moment

Oliver I am going to see if the evening paper has arrived yet. Terry Boswell was kind enough to say that he'd pick one up on the way back from the pub. If you will both excuse me.

Oliver exits, on his dignity

Judith That was a bit unnecessary, wasn't it?
Howard I wasn't going to sit here and let him attack you like that. A new member of my team.
Judith I can look after myself.
Howard I know. I've watched you these last nine weeks at school.
Judith Watched me?
Howard At meetings. In the staffroom. You're building something of a reputation.
Judith As what?
Howard What's the American phrase? A tough cookie.
Judith Oh dear.
Howard I think it's a good thing. Self-possession. Determination. Competence. It's a very attractive combination.
Judith Is it?
Howard Have you finished marking Pat's papers?
Judith Yes.
Howard (*standing*) Why does it always take hours, hours and hours longer than you think?
Judith What?
Howard Marking.
Judith Does it? I finished mine this afternoon.
Howard This afternoon? Judith, you know what? You're amazing.
Judith Am I? How was Gerald Spinks about postponing the meeting this afternoon?
Howard Fine. I've got Gerald Spinks wrapped round my little finger.
Judith Have you?
Howard You know what's most amazing about you? Your poise. That self-possession thing. It's something I've noticed about you at work. The rest of us are rushing around, working to deadlines, moaning about the pressure, tearing our hair out — and you just seem to glide above it all. You're … You make everything seem so effortless.
Judith I've only marked a few exam papers, Howard, not painted the Sistine Chapel ceiling.
Howard You never seem to break into a sweat about anything. I like that. On an attractiveness scale of ten, I give it a nine.
Judith Sweatlessness?
Howard Poise. So what did you get up to this afternoon, while the rest of us were slaving away?
Judith I had a workout in the gym. And a sauna. And at the risk of shattering your tender illusions I sweated like a pig.
Howard Did you?

Judith Howard, is this leading up to something?

Howard I think we both know what it's leading up to. It's there, isn't it? It's all there. From the day I interviewed you, it's been there. You can't deny it's there.

Judith I think you're going to have to give me a small clue.

Howard I don't know — what would you call it? An electricity? A chemistry? From the moment you walked into the interview room. An unmistakable but unspoken agreement, something special shared between us, something that we both know is going to happen, is bound to happen one day...

Judith All this was going on while you asked me how I'd reorganize the book cupboard?

Howard You don't know how hard I found it to concentrate in the interview. God, your perfume — it drives me mad every time you walk past me in the staffroom. It's driving me mad now. Your mouth ... Your breath smells like wine ...

Judith That's because I've been drinking wine.

Howard Delicious ... It smells delicious ... I could get drunk on your breath, on your warm, scented breath ——

Judith Howard, if this is going where it seems to be going, then I have to tell you that it's not. Going. Anywhere.

Howard Not?

Pause

No, that's fine. That's fair enough, of course. That's very clear, you've made it very clear.

Pause

(*Standing and moving away*) So there's no chance at all, then? When do you think it might be, then?

Judith Howard, I don't just jump into bed — especially these beds — with anybody after nine weeks' acquaintance. If anything like that came up, I would need to know somebody, you know, really know them, for a long time.

Howard (*flopping into an armchair*) God, I am so tired. I've had to mark all the *Return of the Native*s as well.

Judith All of them?

Howard Somebody had to. I'm Team Leader, so in the end it all falls on my shoulders. It's the burden of responsibility. It's the ——

Judith Loneliness of command?

Howard What?

Judith I thought you were insisting that Terry Boswell did them?

Howard The man's not worth bothering with. I could have gone in there and shouted and made a scene. He hadn't got a leg to stand on. I could have gone to Gerald Spinks with it. I could have. I'd have won, too, but frankly, Boswell's not worth the emotional energy.

Judith So you've ended up doing nine hours of extra work?

Howard shrugs

Howard Who were you drinking wine with?

Judith Do you mean with whom was I drinking wine?

Howard Oh, God, don't start sounding like ...

Judith If it's any of your business, which I very much doubt, it was with Terry Boswell.

Howard I see.

Judith And Team A.

Howard That sounds cosy.

Judith It was. Terry was showing us his snooker trick shots.

Howard It's bloody typical. Byfleet's up the creek, the cross-path analysis is still to be done and Boswell and Team A spend the whole afternoon in the bar. My God, if Gerald Spinks knew what Boswell gets up to.

Judith I should think he does. He was there as well.

Howard Gerald Spinks?

Judith He laid on the snooker table with a pink in his mouth and Terry Boswell shot it out with a red. Very funny. The Spinks with the pinks, Terry called him. Gerald's got a lot of energy for a man in his sixties. It's very attractive. I do find energy attractive.

Howard (*leaping out of his chair*) It's gone half-past ten! Where's the rest of my team? Half-past ten. I told them! And what's happening about these *Godots*, Judith?

Judith They're ——

Howard This is it, isn't it? This is absolutely bloody it! Terry Boswell and his cronies swan around in the bar ingratiating themselves with Gerald Spinks, while there's still piles of serious work lying around to be done. Well, he's not going to get away with it this time, I don't care if he is shooting balls out of Gerald Spinks' mouth, this time I'm going to ——

Judith They're marked.

Howard What?

Judith They're marked. I reminded Terry this afternoon. He sent somebody along for them and Terry and his team marked them in the bar while you were sulking up in your room.

Howard I wasn't sulking. (*Pause*) I see. Well. Good. You didn't do any of these?

Judith Not a one.

Howard Good. Because you're on my team, not Terry Boswell's!
Judith I spent most of the afternoon talking to Gerald Spinks.
Howard Wasn't that difficult with his mouth full?

Howard checks through the Godot scripts, making sure that Judith has told him the truth; he tuts with disapproval as he goes

Pat enters carrying an enormous pile of papers. She hasn't changed for the evening. She takes in Howard and Judith, moves across to her table and deposits the papers

Finished, Pat?
Pat Yes.
Howard Have you got your interim mark matrix?

Pat hands Howard a sheet of paper and exits through the door she came in through

Good.

Oliver enters. He carries no papers except an evening newspaper, which he is rifling through, worriedly

Oliver Nothing — nothing — nothing ... Good heavens, surely they ... (*He checks rapidly through the whole paper again*) Nothing. Good Lord. I'm in the clear! They haven't put it in, Howard, they haven't put it in!
Howard Lucky, Oliver. Very lucky.

Ian enters with an absolutely huge pile of papers

Oliver Ah, Ian, my dear boy, they haven't put it in! They haven't printed my story! I cannot help but feel that my luck is changing.
Ian It's got nothing to do with luck.
Oliver What do you mean?
Ian You don't teach media studies, do you?
Oliver God forbid. I'm not even certain I know what they are.
Ian (*taking the newspaper from Oliver*) You see? There's that plane crash at Gatwick, speculations about the sex life of yet another bloody bishop and Cherie Blair turning down the *Playboy* centrefold. News values, see? No room left for your little story so it didn't make it across the news threshold.
Oliver Praised be God for it. I cannot help but feel my luck is changing.
Ian Not so lucky for the people on the plane, though, was it?
Oliver I didn't mean for a moment that I ... Is that the sort of thing you teach?

Ian Some of the time.
Oliver Good grief.
Howard Interim mark matrix, Ian.

Ian hands Howard a grubby piece of paper

What have you been doing? Blowing your nose on it?
Ian Only the once.
Oliver Do you want mine, Howard?
Howard Unless you've locked it in the lavatory for safe-keeping, Oliver.
Oliver Touché, touché …

Pat comes in with a huge pile of papers

They haven't printed it, Pat. My reputation is safe, all is well, and all manner of things shall be well.
Pat Oh, Oliver, I am pleased.

Oliver goes out

Howard (*muttering to himself over his sheets*) Aardmann — yes; Cholic … OK; Tostevin — that looks OK. Averaging — bingo! We're done for today, people.

The team members manage a ragged cheer

So, all that remains to do is to transport all this lot to the Library, ready for the full moderation meeting with both teams tomorrow.

The team members groan

All right, all right. Probably best if we do this in an orderly way.

Oliver returns with his papers

Howard takes Oliver's pages and incorporates them with the rest. The room is now full of piles of paper again

(*To Oliver*) You position yourself at the bottom of the stairs and we'll pass the piles down to you.
Oliver Oliver, thank you.
Howard Sorry?
Oliver Nothing.

Howard Ian, you position yourself half-way down the stairs and pass the papers to Oliver.

Judith Wouldn't it be better the other way around?

Howard And why would that be, Judith?

Judith Because the person at the bottom of the stairs has to pick up his pile and walk to the Library. Ian would be quicker.

Ian Thanks very much.

Oliver I might be a stalwart, but I'm not that ancient, you know.

Pat But don't forget your back, Oliver?

Oliver Ah yes, good point. Standing on the stairs receiving papers here, twisting downwind to pass them on to Ian like this —— (*He demonstrates the manoeuvre necessary*) Ouch. I felt a twinge even then …

Howard Could we just get on? Please? Can we just do one simple thing relatively quickly and with no fuss, without turning it into a re-run of the D-Day landings?

Oliver Sorry, I'm sure.

Howard Judith, you take the papers from Pat at the door and pass them along the landing to Oliver. Now can we just do it?

Everybody moves to their positions, which obviously involves Judith, Ian and Oliver leaving the room. As he leaves, Ian starts to whistle the "Hi-Ho" song from Snow White. *Oliver joins in, cheerfully*

Pat stands by the door. Howard positions himself over a pile of papers and picks off a small sheaf, which he passes to Pat; she then hands them out of the door. This is repeated. During the following Howard never takes off more than half a dozen sheets. He passes Pat another tiny pile

Not too heavy for you?

Pat (*puzzled*) No. (*She takes the papers to the door and comes back for another load*)

Howard Pat…

Pat Mmm?

Howard How are you doing?

Pat All right. (*She takes the next pile to the door and returns*)

Howard (*giving Pat another pile*) Good. Good. That's good. You're sure that's not too heavy for you?

Pat Yes. (*She takes the latest pile to the door and returns*)

Howard hands Pat another pile but keeps hold of his end, so that she can't get away

Howard I'm sorry if I've been difficult.

Pat What do you mean — if? (*She pulls the bundle away and goes to the door with it*)

Howard I'm under pressure. You know what I'm like.

Pat I'm learning.

Howard And that's good, isn't it? Learning about each other? All our little moods and foibles.

Howard gives Pat another pile and holds on to it as before, pulling her a little closer this time

Pat Foibles?

Howard Funny word, I know, but I'm in a funny mood. But it is, isn't it? A good thing?

Pat Why? Why is it a good thing?

Howard If we're going to be together.

Pat I thought the point was we weren't going to be together. I thought that was very much your point earlier on.

Howard I didn't say anything earlier on.

Pat Exactly.

Howard So I didn't say no, did I?

Pat You didn't say yes.

Howard But I didn't say no.

Pat No … (*She gently pulls the pile away from him and takes it to the door, then returns to Howard*)

Absently, Howard picks up just a single sheet from the pile and hands it to Pat, still holding on to it himself. They move close together, as if heading for a kiss, during the following

Howard Coming to my room tonight?

Pat I shouldn't think so.

Howard Go on. I'll make you very welcome.

Pat That's what I'm afraid of. Not until we've worked out something more ——

Howard More what?

Pat — long term ——

Howard We could plan the long term while we're enjoying the short term.

Pat Trouble is I think the short term might take my mind off the long term.

Howard Then the long term will have to wait its turn, won't it?

They are very close

Judith enters

Judith Are you moving these papers or re-sitting them?

Pat leaps apart from Howard, ripping the sheet of paper in half

(*Taking in the scene*) And can we have bigger bundles, please, because Grumpy and Dozy would like to get to bed sometime before dawn. And so would I.

Judith turns to go out

Pat wags her finger at Howard, who slaps his wrist exaggeratedly

(*Turning back at the door*) What?
Pat Nothing.

Judith goes

Whistling the "Hi-Ho" tune, Howard picks up an absolutely huge bundle and staggers towards Pat with it. Pat takes the bundle from Howard and, as she does so, he steals a kiss. When she takes the weight she staggers slightly in surprise at it

Whoops! What are you doing, Howard?
Howard You heard Eva Peron. Anyway, she's not the only one who's eager to go to bed.

Pat starts whistling the "Hi-Ho" tune. Howard joins in. They whistle it in between their bits of dialogue during the following. From here on Howard picks up bigger bundles and the bulk of the papers gets moved quite quickly, though the effort takes a toll on both of them

Pat You know, for a while there ... for a moment ...
Howard What?
Pat I thought that you had your sights set on ...
Howard Who?
Pat You know ... (*She jerks her head to indicate outside the door, nearly losing her footing under her enormous pile as she does so*)

During Howard's following speech, Oliver wanders in

Howard Eva Braun? Oh, Pat, really, credit me with some taste ... Name this play in one. (*He pretends to sink under the weight of his pile of papers and speaks in a terrible American woman's accent*) "They say he give them but two words. 'More weight,' he says. And died. 'More weight'." (*In a deep, terrible American man's accent*) "More weight."

Pat laughs

Oliver *The Crucible*, Act Four. Set text for what seemed like an eternity. Rather like the play itself.
Howard (*breathless by now*) I thought you were on the stairs?
Oliver I was, but young master Ian said I was too slow and I was holding him up. He sent me up here to help you.
Howard Grab hold of a pile, then, and we'll feed Pat.

They work away during the following, whistling and getting more and more out of breath

Oliver I can't tell you how relieved I feel about all that newspaper business. Quite a relief. Would have quite shot my reputation in the local community. And at the school, of course. By the by, I've arranged to have them picked up from Portsmouth by courier. They'll be here by the morning. What with taxis and couriers, this weekend is costing me more than the pittance I'll earn.

They finish moving the papers, overloading Pat now that she has a continuous conveyor belt to cope with. They are all totally breathless by the end

Ian staggers into the room, wheezing and gasping, almost entirely unable to catch his breath

Ian My God … I've got to give up the recreational drugs.

They all stand or sit around, bent over, chests heaving for breath

Judith walks coolly into the room, totally poised and not at all out of breath

Judith Is that it?

Howard manages to nod

Good-night, then. Pat. Oliver. Howard. Good-night, Ian.
Ian 'Night.

Judith goes

The others just stand or sit as they were, their breathing subsiding

Ay, well, that's me, as my mother used to say. As if we didn't know already.

Howard Not going to the bar, Ian?

Ian Not tonight. Totally knackered, mate. See you all.

Ian exits

Howard and Pat sit there. Oliver also sits, oblivious

Howard (*eventually, slapping his knee*) Yes, well, I think I'll be going up myself.

Oliver Yes, yes. Good idea.

Howard Have they given you the same room this year, Oliver?

Oliver Oh yes. With the view of the laurels. I like that room.

Howard Yes, I've got the same room. The same room as last year.

Oliver How about you, Pat, have you…

Pat No, I've got a different one.

Howard Right. I'm off. Yes, the room at the end of the corridor, Oliver. The same as last year. Night.

Howard exits

Oliver Extraordinary man.

Pat Hmm?

Oliver He hardly deigns to speak to me all day, except to be rude, and then goes to great lengths to describe the whereabouts of his room to me.

Pat Yes. Oh well, good-night, Oliver.

Oliver Good-night, Pat. You get a good night's sleep. You need it.

Pat Yes.

Oliver The last thing you want after a day like yours is to be tossing and turning and thrashing about all night.

Pat looks at the door Howard has just left through and looks guilty. Something twigs in Oliver and he puts two and two together

   Oh.

Pat Please don't say anything, Oliver.

Oliver Oh well, you've made your bed, you'll just have to lie … (*He clears his throat*)

Pat Good-night, then.

Oliver Yes. Good-night. Sleep tight. Don't let the… (*He clears his throat*)

Pat goes out

   Well, well. Well, well, well. Disappointing.

Oliver sits there, alone. He stares into space. He looks at his watch. He plumps up the cushions on the sofa. Eventually, he gets up and wanders round the room. Perhaps he mutters to himself. He picks up a book, looks at it, discards it. He picks up a tatty sensational paperback and Howard's copy of The Compendium of Marking Guidelines. *He wrinkles his nose at the paperback and decides on the guidelines and sits down to read. He reads quietly for a few moments, sinking comfortably into the chair. Then something makes him stiffen and he quickly slides back up again. He puts the book down on his knees and thinks to himself, his lips moving. His eyes brighten. He checks the book again, then stands, moving rapidly to the other side of the room. He picks up the green marking instruction sheet and checks the book. He picks up the pink marking instruction sheet and checks the book. A smile begins to spread across his face. He thinks, furiously, then crosses to the phone. He stabs out a number*

(*Into the phone*) Is that the bar? Is Gerald Spinks there, if you please? Thank you. (*He waits a few moments, humming*) Hallo, Gerald? It's Oliver Goldsmith. ... No, no relation. Gerald I wondered if perchance you had Howard's — what do you call them — little bleeper thing — pager, that's it — would you have his pager number at all? ... You have? Thank you. ... Yes, yes, I've got that. So if I ring that it'll just bleep and go on bleeping, will it? ... Until he cancels it. Yes, that's right, Gerald, a bit of a wheeze. You know what we boys are like. ... Right you are, Gerald. ... And a good-night to you, sir. (*He hangs up, waits a moment, then gleefully dials again. He puts the receiver down, wanders across to the table, picks up the two pieces of marking scheme paper — one green, one pink — and examines them*)

After a few moments a continuous bleep is heard from the corridor. It gradually makes its way nearer and eventually the door flies open and Howard storms in in a state of disarray. He is glaring at his bleeping pager whilst trying to tie up the string of his pyjama bottoms and pull a woman's dressing-gown around himself

Howard This had better be bloody important, Oliver, because I was in the middle of ...
Oliver Middle of what, Howard?
Howard Something important.
Oliver (*holding up the pieces of paper and moving them backwards and forwards alternately*) Pink or green, Howard? Pink or green or green or pink? Pink, green, pink, green. Which?
Howard What is this? Some kind of demented origami lesson?
Oliver Pink or green or green or pink? Which is which?

Howard You've cracked under the pressure. I'm going back to bed. (*He moves to the door*)
Oliver You're colour blind, aren't you?
Howard What?
Oliver I said you're colour blind, aren't you, Howard?

Pat enters from the same door as Howard and stands listening. She is wearing a man's dressing-gown

Howard No, I'm not.
Oliver Yes you are.
Howard I'm not.
Oliver You are, you know.
Howard Not.
Oliver Then tell me which is which: which one's pink and which one's green?
Howard Look, I don't have to play your stupid games, Oliver ——
Oliver Colour blind.
Howard All right: (*he gets it wrong*) that's the pink and that's the green.

Oliver just stands looking at Howard

No, that's the pink and that's... (*But he realizes it's too late*) All right, so I'm a bit colour blind, but I don't see what difference that makes or why you had to drag me out of bed to —— (*And then the penny drops*) Oh no.
Pat I was using the right guidelines all along.
Oliver Correct.
Pat And all that re-marking of my work we did this afternoon ——
Oliver — was utterly academic. No pun intended.
Pat (*picking up a handful of papers*) So it wasn't my fault? I was right and you were wrong. (*She hits him with the papers*) And you still made me feel about this big. You made me apologize, and I did, and everybody thought "Poor old Pat" and I felt so guilty and — and — and it was your fault all along, you bastard, you bastard, you self-opinionated, arrogant —— (*She rains blows on him*)
Howard Pat, Pat, now stop it, stop it! Ow! Stop it, Pat! Control yourself, woman!
Pat You're no better than my bloody husband!
Howard Who's got a good deal more sense than I credited him with. If I was in his place I'd get the children away from you, too, you're a bloody mad woman ——
Pat You shit! Don't you dare to talk about my children! Don't you dare presume to say anything about how I raise them! Don't you dare! (*She hits him really quite hard*)

Oliver (*who is really enjoying this and not lifting a finger to help Howard*)
Now, now. Come along, come along, Pat. Violence is never the answer.
Not the done thing to kick a man when he's down.

Pat calms down, all her energy spent, during the following

Howard (*to Oliver*) I don't know why you're looking so pleased with
yourself.
Oliver Don't you? Well, I do have my reasons, take my word for it. Years
and years of reasons. Good-night. (*He starts for the door*)
Howard Where are you going?
Oliver To my bed. To sleep the sleep of the just.
Howard I don't think you've thought through the implications of this.
Oliver I think I have. And I'm enjoying every one of them.
Howard Including the one that means that we're going to have to do a total
re-mark? Of everything? Before the meeting tomorrow morning? I thought
that might give you pause, you pompous prat.
Oliver But you can't be serious! I can't stay awake for that long marking
some spotty oik's ramblings on the pathetic fallacy in Wordsworth. It's
inhuman. It's psychological torture!
Howard You should have thought of that before you paged me. Pat, get the
others down. Pat.
Pat Bastard.

Pat goes

Oliver As a matter of fact, I paged you because an error had occurred. The
integrity of the exam was in question. I was acting at the urging of my
professional conscience.
Howard Bollocks. You did it because you've never been able to stand the
sight of me and you hate my guts.
Oliver That may have formed a minor part of the equation, certainly.

Pat returns. She looks slightly shocked but not unhappy

Howard Did you rouse them?
Pat Hardly necessary.
Howard Are you all right?
Pat Oh yes. No problem. Not for me, anyway.
Howard Pat …

*Judith enters. She is in elegant nightwear, but looks slightly dishevelled,
certainly not her normal immaculate self*

Judith Well?

Howard Yes. The thing is, Judith, there's been a slight hiccup, that is to say ——

Pat The shit has hit the fan in no uncertain terms.

Howard Not exactly, not exactly, but the fact is that because of a technical oversight ——

Pat snorts

—— we have to undertake a certain amount of rearrangement, reconsideration...

Oliver We have to re-mark the entire sample.

Judith I hope that's a joke.

Oliver Alas ...

Judith Whose fault is it this time?

Pat Don't look at me.

Howard It's a simple misunderstanding. It could happen to anyone.

Oliver Anyone who's colour blind.

Judith You used the wrong mark sheet.

Howard Broadly speaking.

Judith Incredible. Utterly incredible.

Howard Now, we can quite easily get over this little problem if ——

Oliver There's modern management for you. When I mislay my papers it's akin to a nuclear accident. When Pat slips up it's a hanging offence. But when you create another twelve hours' work it's a little problem!

Judith I wouldn't grace it with the word management. Perhaps this isn't the moment to say it, but —— no it is, it is exactly the moment to say it —— I've been marking papers for twelve years now and never, never have I come across such a mind-boggling degree of managerial balls-up as I have in the last twelve hours.

Pat But I thought you said you worked for Howard?

Howard That's enough, Pat. All right, Judith, you've had your say, but now, as your line manager, I'm saying to you that ——

Judith You do flatter yourself, Howard. You couldn't draw a line, let alone manage one.

Howard If you've got any complaints, Judith, you can take them to Gerald Spinks.

Judith (*after a momentary hesitation*) There'll be no need for that.

Howard (*slightly taken aback*) Oh. Good. Good. That's excellent. I always think it's best to resolve these things within the team. Now, our first task, obviously, is to get the papers back up here. Oliver, you get them out of the library and up the stairs.

Oliver Oh those stairs again.

Howard Ian can … Where is Ian? Pat, did you see Ian?
Pat Yes. I think he was just coming.
Howard Good. Well, until he comes you bring the piles into here and Judith
and I will sort them. And Oliver, Pat: quietly.
Pat Why?
Howard It's eleven o'clock. People will be asleep.

Oliver and Pat head for the exit

Oliver (*in a loud whisper*) He doesn't want Gerald Spinks to know.
Howard I heard that, Oliver.
Oliver Good.

Oliver and Pat exit

Howard That was a bit unnecessary, I thought.

Judith shrugs

I was hoping we could build a working relationship based on mutual trust.
Judith Doesn't that have to be earned?
Howard A bit cheap, wasn't it? Very unprofessional, attacking me in front
of my staff? Trying to diminish me in their eyes.
Judith Oh, I'm good, Howard. I know I'm good. But not even I can perform
the impossible.

*Pat staggers in with a huge pile of papers. She looks around, blithely
innocent, obviously enjoying the tense atmosphere, and goes out again*

Howard and Judith sort the papers into smaller piles during the following

Howard What's he offered you, then?
Judith Who?
Howard Who? I wasn't born yesterday, you know.
Judith I've got no idea what you're talking about.
Howard Him. The one with the nice eyes.
Judith Terry Boswell?

Pat comes in with another huge pile

Howard and Judith lapse into silence

Pat goes out

Howard Made you an offer you couldn't refuse, did he?
Judith To do what? What are you talking about?
Howard To sabotage my team.
Judith To … This is unbelievable.
Howard To undermine my authority, destabilize everything I've worked
for …
Judith I only met the man this morning!

*Pat comes in again with a large pile of papers. She dumps the papers and
goes out*

Howard What did he offer you? To infiltrate my team?
Judith You're deluded! What do you think this is? We're marking A level
papers, Howard, not reliving the Cold War!
Howard So what was it? His deputy when he finally sticks his nose far
enough up Gerald Spinks' backside to get the Chief Examinership?

*Oliver plods in, holding a small pile of papers. He stands watching,
fascinated and pleased*

Judith Can you hear yourself, Howard?
Howard And what did you offer him in return?
Judith What did you say?
Howard I said what did you offer him in return?
Judith I hope you're not going to say what I think you're going to say.

Pat staggers in with a huge pile of papers and stands watching

Howard I've met women like you before. On the make. On the up. Sleep
with anyone to get where you want to go.

*Judith moves swiftly towards Howard and slaps him hard around the face.
Howard's face collapses and he looks as if he is going to cry. Oliver and Pat
look on, appalled, but with pleasure mixed in there somewhere, too*

Oliver (*after clearing his throat*) Howard, this may not be quite the moment,
but we just bumped into Gerald Spinks in the bar. He'd like a word.

*Howard rocks on his heels for a moment, and then, with a decisive sniff,
is gone*

The remaining three stand around, awkwardly

Oliver Fancy a glass of hot milk and a digestive, Pat?
Pat Yes.

Oliver and Pat put down their piles of papers and slip quietly out

Judith stands still

After a moment the far door bursts open and Ian is there, triumphant, dressed only in a very small single duvet

Ian Scots w'hae!
Judith What are you doing? I told you to stay upstairs until I came back.
Ian You should never stop a Scotsman in mid-stride. It plays havoc with his sporran. Did you not know that?
Judith Ian, get back upstairs. Somebody'll see you.
Ian S'all right. I'll tell them it's my family tartan.
Judith Idiot.

Ian tries to embrace Judith, but she manages to slide away from him

Ian Do you often go round doing that? Seducing younger men.
Judith I haven't seduced you yet.
Ian Just a boring technicality.
Judith Don't get too excited. We've got to do a full re-mark.
Ian Tonight? What for? No. Stupid question, Ian. Howard's made a balls.
Judith That's right.
Ian Jesus, that man. I don't know how you work for him.
Judith I don't think I will be for much longer. By the way, how do you manage to look scruffy, even when you've got no clothes on?
Ian It's genetic.
Judith What is it with male teachers and scruffiness? I work in a staffroom that resembles a meeting of the Worzel Gummidge Society. And now there's you.
Ian If I'm such a scruffbag, why are we going to have an affair?
Judith We're not.
Ian Sorry. I'm a bit lost here. Didn't you come to my room just now, and ——
Judith We're not going to have an affair. You can't afford it.
Ian What, are you telling me you charge for it or something?
Judith I'll ignore that because you're young and overexcited. What can you offer me, Ian? Expensive hotels? Weeks away in the Caribbean?
Ian Chemistry. I can offer you chemistry. It's there. You know it. I know it. We both knew it straight away this morning.

Judith What about my husband?

Ian I don't know. I've never met him. Would we have chemistry do you think? (*He starts to laugh, sees her face and stops*)

Judith I'm not going to leave him. And I'm not going to mess myself or our marriage up having an affair.

Ian Rich, is he?

Judith He's an entrepreneur.

Ian One of those.

Judith I used to say that. Until I sat down and worked out that what I'd spent on clothes that year was roughly equivalent to my total net salary. Everything else — the house, the car, the restaurants, the holidays — it all came from him. He gives me everything else I need. Nearly everything else I need.

Ian What doesn't he give you?

Judith I thought I'd answered that upstairs.

Ian You could live without all those other things.

Judith Of course I could. The question is, do I want to?

Ian moves to Judith and kisses her

Ian So this is just another one of those young man's sweaty three o'clock in the morning wish fulfilment jobs?

Judith You get a lot of this, do you?

Ian Happens to me all the time.

Judith I don't want the commitment of an affair. But we can see each other. Now and then. If you want.

Ian When?

Judith There are courses. Lots of courses. Weekends. Things like this, once or twice a year. If you want.

Ian kisses Judith again and they sink into a settee. Ian pulls the duvet over them. Judith giggles and her hand appears, holding a clutch of papers

The door flies open and Howard enters, distraught

Howard That's it, then! That's bloody it! They're not giving me the Chief Examinership! After all my years of selfless devotion to this examining board, the years of grinding, boring graft, they're not giving me the Chief Examinership. (*He comes into the room and slams the door to. He passes the settee, absently and automatically taking the papers from Judith's hand and tidying the edges, but is in such a lather that he does not take in what is going on. He does as the speech progresses, however*) Happy now, Judith? Your mate Terry Boswell will assume the crown after years of well-planned strategic inactivity. It's enough to make you want to — to make you want to ... (*He takes in Judith and Ian together*)

Oliver and Pat arrive in the doorway and take the scene in, too. There is more than a moment of rather deadly silence

Oliver What's the etiquette of a moment like this, I wonder?

Howard eventually snaps. With a huge cry he flings the papers in his hand at Judith and Ian. He moves round the room picking up more and more paper and throwing it at people as he does so

Howard Betrayed everywhere I turn! By you! (*He flings papers at Judith and Ian*) By you! (*He flings papers at Pat*) And as for you (*Oliver*)... you pompous, self-regarding windbag, I've put up with years of your overblown, self-opinionated upper-middle class garbage. (*He flings some papers at Oliver. He turns his attention back to Judith, flinging papers as he shouts*) And haven't you got any taste? Eh? A man who has string in his shoes for shoelaces?

Ian Don't get me angry, pal.

Howard (*mimicking Judith*) "I ... have to know somebody really well before I ..." How long have you known this scruffbag, eh?

Ian Right. I'm angry. That's it. (*He picks up a handful of papers and flings them at Howard*)

Howard (*flinging paper back*) Five minutes? Ten? And then you're at it like rabbits ... Why him? Eh? Why him and not me? Eh?

Judith Because his knees don't crack when he stands up and his backside isn't hanging round his kneecaps.

Howard You're bloody shameless ...

Judith I can get all that at home.

Pat Howard ...

Howard Get away from me ... (*He flings more papers at Pat*)

Oliver You don't treat a lady like that in my presence!

Howard Oh shut up, you old woman!

Oliver Very well! So be it!

Oliver, furious, picks up papers and throws them, underarm, during the following. Pat feeds him with ammunition. Howard is by now throwing papers at everybody, and they are throwing them at him. Only Judith refrains. There is a veritable snowstorm of paper and their shouting reaches a cacophony

Howard (*to Judith*) But the thing that really disgusts me, that really, really disgusts me is you and Terry Boswell!

Judith, fairly impassive, stares at Howard

Fluttering your eyelashes and your Janet Regers at him, just to get to be his deputy! And you lecture me about being a professional? My God!

Judith (*snapping at this last comment; shouting*) You stupid man. You can't even get hysteria right. You think I have to flirt with someone like Terry Boswell to get on? I'm insulted. You idiot. Terry Boswell's going to the Northern Board as Chief Executive. As you'd know if you ever spoke to him.

The paperfighting subsides as Judith's speech sinks into Howard. Eventually the battle stops as much through exhaustion as anything else

Howard Chief Executive? But then ... So who's going to ... I mean ... The Chief Examiner here?

Judith It's yet to be decided. All I'll say is that I'm having breakfast with Gerald Spinks. And now I'm going back to bed. You'll clear this up, Howard. And then there's the re-mark. On a scale of things to do before tomorrow morning, that's about a ten, I should think. Good-night.

Judith exits

There is a rather awkward silence. After a while, Ian stands up, pulling his duvet round him

Ian Ay, well — I'd better ... Early start in the morning.

Ian moves off, rather shamefacedly, his duvet dragging behind him. He does the door opening trick with his foot and goes out

There is another awkward silence

Oliver Goodbye to literature and all that. Hallo communications skills, performance criteria and the mirthless grimace of an appropriate response to humour. Oh, brave new world.

Pat "The worst is not, so long as we can say 'This is the worst'."

The phone rings. Oliver answers it

Oliver (*into the phone*) ... Yes. Speaking. ... No. Certainly not. (*He hangs up*) Local television company. They're running the missing papers story for breakfast television tomorrow. Did I wish to appear to put my side of the case? And now I have a problem. Who do I hand my resignation letter to? (*He catches himself*) I apologize. To whom do l hand my letter of resignation?

Oliver stands still for a moment, thinking, then exits

Pat and Howard are left alone. Howard fills up and is about to cry. He holds out his hand to Pat

Howard Pat ...

Pat pulls a handkerchief from her sleeve, hands it to Howard none too gently and exits

Howard blows his nose and recovers slightly. Absently, he reaches out for the nearest sheaf of papers and begins to tidy them. He starts to laugh, a little disturbingly. The laugh becomes more frenzied, as does the tidying process, and soon he is flinging torn and tattered papers into the air. He hurls himself around the room yelling and laughing manically

The Lights fade

FURNITURE AND PROPERTY LIST

ACT I

On stage: Leather armchairs
Sofa. *On it*: cushions
Hatstand
Municipal plastic chairs
School laminated tables. *On one*: telephone. *On another*: folder of transparencies. *On another*: two piles of exam papers, one large, one small; marking sheet; pink marking band guidelines sheet and pen for **Pat**
Books, including tatty sensational paperback and "The Compendium of Marking Guidelines"

Off stage: Thirteen piles of papers (**Ian** and **Howard**)
Clipboard (**Howard**)
Overhead projection machine — practical (**Judith**)
Overhead projection machine, briefcase (**Oliver**)
Single sheet of paper (**Ian**)
Cup of tea, plate, Danish pastry (**Oliver**)
Cups of tea, plates, cakes (**Oliver** and **Pat**)

Personal: **Howard**: pager, pen, marking sheet, green marking band guidelines sheet
Oliver: stick of chalk, wallet containing neatly folded sheet of paper, half-moon reading glasses, green marking band guidelines sheet, watch (worn throughout)
Judith: marking sheet, green marking band guidelines sheet
Ian: marking sheet, green marking band guidelines sheet, watch (worn throughout)
Pat: handkerchief

ACT II

Set: Papers strewn around room
Howard's papers on table

Strike: **Pat**'s papers from table

Off stage: Six enormous piles of papers (**Pat**)
                  Huge pile of papers (**Ian**)
                  Evening newspaper (**Oliver**)
                  Papers (**Oliver**)
                  Very small single duvet (**Ian**)
                  Large pile of papers (**Judith**)
                  Small pile of papers (**Oliver**)

LIGHTING PLOT

Property and practical fittings required: nil
One interior. The same throughout

ACT I

To open: General interior lighting

Cue 1   **Ian**: " *... Return of the* bloody *Native*." Groans all round   (Page 35)
              Black-out

ACT II

To open: General interior lighting

Cue 2   **Howard** hurls himself around, yelling and laughing   (Page 60)
              Fade lights to black-out

EFFECTS PLOT

ACT I

ACT II